Animal Top Tens

Europe's Most Amazing Animals

Anita Ganeri

Raintree

Chicago, Illinois

Photo Research: Mica Brancic
Editorial: Nancy Dickmann and Catherine Veitch
Design: Victoria Bevan and Geoff Ward
Illustrations: Geoff Ward
Production: Victoria Fitzgerald

Originated by Modern Age
Printed and bound by CTPS (China Translation & Printing Services Ltd)

12 11 10 09 08
10 9 8 7 6 5 4 3 2 1

Library of Congress Cataloging-in-Publication Data
Ganeri, Anita, 1961-
  Europe's most amazing animals / Anita Ganeri.
    p. cm. -- (Animal top tens)
  Includes bibliographical references and index.
  ISBN 978-1-4109-3086-6 (hc) -- ISBN 978-1-4109-3095-8 (pb) 1. Animals--Europe--Juvenile literature. I. Title.
  QL253.G36 2008
  591.94--dc22
                                2007047552

7/10

Acknowledgments
The author and publisher are grateful to the following for permission to reproduce copyright material: ©Alamy/ blickwinkel/Hecker p. **14**; ©Ardea pp. **4** (Steffen & Alexandra Sailer), **6** (John Cancalosi), **7** (Stefan Meyers), **8** (Pascal Goetgheluck), **12** (Duncan Usher), **21** (Piers Cavendish); ©FLPA pp. **11** (Derek Middleton), **19** (Chris Mattison), **20** (Jurgen & Christine Sohns); ©FLPA/ Foto Natura Stock p. **25**; ©FLPA/Minden Pictures/JH Editorial p. **17** (Cyril Ruoso); Naturepl p. **10** (Dietmar Nill) [OSF]; ©OSF pp. **16** (Juniors Bildarchiv), **18** (Mike Linley), **22** (Manfred Pfefferle), **23** (Emanuele Biggi), **24** (Rodger Jackman), **27** (Antinolo Jorge Sierra); ©OSF/ Mauritius Die Bildagentur Gmbh pp. **9** (Rauschenbach), **15** (DHerrmann Dherrmann), **26** (Pölking Pölking); ©OSF/Robert Harding Picture Library Ltd p. **13** (Steve & Ann Toon).

Cover photograph of a European eagle owl, reproduced with permission of PhotoLibrary/Juniors Bildarchiv.

The publisher would like to thank Michael Bright for his assistance in the preparation of this book.

Every effort has been made to contact copyright holders of any material reproduced in this book. Any omissions will be rectified in subsequent printings if notice is given to the publishers.

Contents

Some words are printed in bold, **like this**. You can find out what they mean in the Glossary.

Europe

Europe is the second smallest **continent**, covering just over 4 million square miles (10 million square kilometers). Only Australasia is smaller than Europe. Europe stretches from Spain and Portugal in the west, to Russia in the east. To the north there is Scandinavia. To the south there is the Mediterranean Sea.

Europe has many different types of landscapes. A curve of mountains roughly divides the cooler north from the warmer south. Huge forests of fir and pine trees stretch across the far north. Further south are large grassy open spaces, mountains, and **woodlands**. Around the Mediterranean Sea, the weather is hot and dry.

Woodlands of **broadleaved** trees are home to many animals.

This map shows some of the main landscapes of Europe.

Iceland

N
W—E
S

Atlantic Ocean

North Sea

Scandinavia

Baltic Sea

Russia

British Isles

Denmark

EUROPE

Alps

Danube River

Black Sea

Portugal

Spain

Mediterranean Sea

Key
■ forest
■ mountains
— river

Europe

0 — 500 miles
0 — 500 kilometers

An amazing range of animals has **adapted** to live in these different **habitats.** Birds, deer, and wild cats live around the Danube River where it flows into the sea. The forests are home to wood ants and many types of birds. Goats and rare brown bears live in the mountains of southern Europe. These animals all have special features to help them survive in their particular homes.

Wild Boar

The wild boar is a large pig, with dark brown, bristly hair. It is active at **dawn** and **dusk** when it searches for food. It uses its long snout to search among the leaves on the forest floor for nuts, **fungi**, roots, mice, and snails.

WILD BOAR

BODY LENGTH:
5–6 FT. (1.5–1.8 M)

WEIGHT:
100–450 LBS
(50–200 KG)

LIFESPAN:
15–20 YEARS

HABITAT:
WOODLANDS

THAT'S AMAZING!:
WILD BOARS LOVE TO WALLOW IN MUD POOLS. THEY DO THIS TO COOL DOWN AND GET RID OF IRRITATING **INSECTS**.

where wild boar live

North Sea

Atlantic Ocean

Europe

Mediterranean Sea

Male boars have two upward-pointing tusks that are extra-large teeth.

Woodlands
Temperate woodlands grow in places that have warm summers and mild winters. The trees are mostly **broadleaved** trees, such as oak, beech, and silver birch. They are mostly deciduous, which means that they lose their leaves in winter.

Family groups

Wild boar piglets are born in a den under a pile of rocks or a fallen tree. The piglets have brown and tan stripes to **camouflage** them among the trees. They live with their mothers and other females and their young. These large groups are called sounders.

Stag Beetle

The stag beetle is the largest beetle in Europe. It lives among oak, ash, and elm trees. Males use their jaws in fights with other males when they are trying to find a female to **mate** with. The loser gets tipped upside down on its back. It then flips itself back over and runs away.

STAG BEETLE

BODY LENGTH:
1–3 IN. (2.5–7.5 CM)

WEIGHT:
ABOUT 0.07 OZ (2 G)

LIFESPAN:
UP TO 7 YEARS

HABITAT:
WOODLANDS

THAT'S AMAZING!:
A STAG BEETLE'S GIANT JAWS ARE USELESS FOR CHEWING. SCIENTISTS ARE NOT SURE IF ADULT STAG BEETLES EAT ANYTHING AT ALL.

where stag beetles live

North Sea

Atlantic Ocean

Europe

Mediterranean Sea

This **insect** gets its name from the male's huge jaws, which look like a deer's antlers.

Life cycle

Stag beetles live in **woodlands**. They need a large supply of dead wood. The female lays her eggs in rotting logs or the stumps of dead trees. When the **larvae** hatch, they feed on the dead wood. They have strong jaws for tearing and chewing. But the wood does not contain many **nutrients** to help the larvae grow. It takes larvae up to seven years to become adults.

Two male stag beetles about to lock jaws in a fight.

Noctule Bat

The noctule bat is one of the largest bats in Europe. It has short, reddish-brown fur, and wide, triangular wings. Noctule bats live in **woodlands** where there are hollow trees. They use the trees for roosting, raising their young, and **hibernating**. They leave their roosts at **dusk** to search for moths, beetles, and other flying **insects**, which they catch in the air and eat.

NOCTULE BAT

BODY LENGTH:
2–3 IN. (5–8 CM)

WEIGHT:
0.6–1.4 OZ (18–40 G)

LIFESPAN:
UP TO 12 YEARS

HABITAT:
WOODLANDS

THAT'S AMAZING!:
A BABY NOCTULE BAT CAN FLY WHEN IT IS FOUR WEEKS OLD.

where noctule bats live

North Sea

Atlantic Ocean

Europe

Mediterranean Sea

Noctule bats fly fast and high above the ground.

Winter sleep

In winter, when the weather is cold and there isn't much to eat, some bats in Europe fly to warmer places further south. Others find a hole in a tree and fall into a deep sleep, called hibernation. During hibernation, the bats sometimes sit on top of each other for warmth.

In summer, noctule bats roost in holes in hollow trees.

Migration
Many animals make long journeys between their breeding and feeding grounds. This is called migration. It lets them take advantage of the best weather and food supplies.

European Eagle Owl

The eagle owl is the largest owl in Europe. It lives in open **woodlands** with rocky areas. It roosts in the trees during the day and makes its nest in cracks in the rocks. The eagle owl has a large beak, enormous **talons**, bright orange eyes, and long, fluffy ear tufts.

EUROPEAN EAGLE OWL

BODY LENGTH:
27 IN. (70 CM)

WEIGHT:
9 LBS (4.1 KG)

LIFESPAN:
UP TO 40 YEARS

HABITAT:
WOODLANDS, ROCKY AREAS

THAT'S AMAZING!:
HOURS AFTER AN OWL HAS EATEN A MEAL, IT VOMITS UP A PELLET OF BONES AND OTHER PIECES OF ITS PREY THAT IT CANNOT DIGEST.

where European eagle owls live

North Sea

Atlantic Ocean

Europe

Mediterranean Sea

The owl's large eyes help it find its prey at night.

The owl's wings are fringed with feathers to help it fly silently.

Forest hunter

The eagle owl is a powerful **bird of prey**. It searches for **prey** at **dusk** and in the early evening. It kills woodland animals, from small deer to mice. It swoops down on its victim, grabs it in its talons and flies off with it in its beak. Small animals are swallowed whole. Larger animals are torn apart. The eagle owl has superb eyesight and hearing for finding its prey in the dark.

Alpine Salamander

The Alpine salamander is a shiny black **amphibian**. It lives in mountain forests and spends the day hiding in **burrows** or cracks in the rocks. At night, it leaves its hiding place to search for beetles, spiders, and centipedes to eat.

ALPINE SALAMANDER

BODY LENGTH:
3.5–5.5 IN (9–14 CM)

WEIGHT:
0.5 OZ (15 G)

LIFESPAN:
10 YEARS

HABITAT:
MOUNTAINS

THAT'S AMAZING!:
TO AVOID THE COLD WEATHER AND LACK OF FOOD IN WINTER, ALPINE SALAMANDERS **HIBERNATE** FOR 6–8 MONTHS OF THE YEAR.

where alpine salamanders live

North Sea

Atlantic Ocean

Europe

Mediterranean Sea

The Alpine salamander lives at heights of up to 10,000 feet (3,000 meters) in the Alps.

Young Alpine salamanders look like miniature versions of their parents.

Mountain survival

The Alpine salamander has some very unusual features to help it survive in the cold, dry mountains. Most amphibians lay eggs in the water. The eggs hatch into fish-like tadpoles. Alpine salamanders give birth to live young. This means that their young avoid the danger of their pond freezing over or drying up. The young stay inside their mother for up to three years before they are born. This protects them from the harsh conditions and also from **predators**.

Alpine Marmot

Alpine marmots are large squirrels that live in the mountains of central and southern Europe. The marmots are active during the day, when they feed mostly on grass, flowers, seeds, and bulbs.

An Alpine marmot has thick fur, a short tail, and small ears.

ALPINE MARMOT

BODY LENGTH:
20–28 IN. (53–73 CM)

WEIGHT:
9–18 LBS (4–8 KG)

LIFESPAN:
4–5 YEARS

HABITAT:
MOUNTAINS

THAT'S AMAZING!:
ALPINE MARMOTS WARN EACH OTHER OF DANGER, SUCH AS EAGLES OR FOXES NEARBY, BY WHISTLING A WARNING.

where alpine marmots live

North Sea

Atlantic Ocean

Europe

Mediterranean Sea

Winter sleep

In summer, Alpine marmots eat as much food as possible. Then they spend six or seven months **hibernating**, huddling together for warmth. The last marmot in the **burrow** plugs up the entrance with dirt and droppings to keep out the cold. The marmots live off their stores of fat until spring comes.

Alpine marmots live in burrows that they dig out with their strong paws and claws.

Hibernation

Winter is a difficult time for animals. The weather is cold and food is scarce. Some animals survive by hibernating. Their body temperature drops, and their heart and breathing rates slow down. They sleep very deeply until the weather gets warmer in spring.

Mallorcan Midwife Toad

The Mallorcan midwife toad lives in the mountains of northern Mallorca (an island off the east coast of Spain). It is well **adapted** to the difficult conditions. Its body is flat so that it can squeeze into cracks in the rocks where it hides during the day. It comes out at night to feed on **insects** that it catches with its long, sticky tongue.

The toad's golden-colored skin provides good **camouflage**.

MIDWIFE TOAD

BODY LENGTH:
UP TO 1.5 IN. (38 MM)

LIFESPAN:
10 YEARS

HABITAT:
MOUNTAINS

THAT'S AMAZING!:
THE TOAD'S BACK IS COVERED IN SMALL WARTS. THE WARTS GIVE OFF A STRONG-SMELLING POISON IF THE TOAD IS ATTACKED.

where midwife toads live

North Sea

Atlantic Ocean

Europe

Mallorca

Mediterranean Sea

The male toad carries the eggs until they hatch to protect them from **predators**.

Caring parents

Midwife toads are unusual because the male toad takes care of the eggs. The female lays strings of eggs that the male wraps around his back legs. When the eggs are ready to hatch, the male wades into the water and lets the tadpoles jump out. Since water is often scarce in the toad's **habitat**, this gives the tadpoles a pool to grow in.

Peregrine Falcon

The peregrine falcon is a **bird of prey** with long, pointed wings and a short tail. Males have gray backs with striped chests. Females are larger and darker. The peregrine falcon lives in marshes, on farmland, and along rocky coasts. It lays its eggs in hollow trees or on rocky ledges. Its **habitat** provides it with plenty of open space for finding **prey.**

Falcons have strong, hooked beaks.

PEREGRINE FALCON

BODY LENGTH:
13–20 IN. (34–50 CM)

WEIGHT:
1–3 LBS (0.5–1.5 KG)

LIFESPAN:
15 YEARS

HABITAT:
MARSHES, FARMLAND, ROCKY SEA COASTS

THAT'S AMAZING!:
PEREGRINES **MATE** FOR LIFE AND RETURN TO THE SAME NESTING SITE YEAR AFTER YEAR.

where peregrines live

North Sea

Atlantic Ocean

Europe

Mediterranean Sea

The way the peregrine dives down on prey is called stooping.

Speedy flier

The peregrine falcon is a high-speed **predator**. When it is chasing prey in the air, it can reach speeds of up to 125 miles (200 kilometers) per hour. This makes it one of the fastest flying birds. It mostly feeds on other birds, such as pigeons. It spots its prey from a distance, then closes its wings and dives down for the kill.

Grass Snake

Grass snakes live in damp places, such as grassy river banks, ditches, and ponds. They are well **adapted** to their **habitat**. The snake's skin is gray-green with black and yellow markings. This **camouflages** it among the long grass. The snake is a very good swimmer and searches for its **prey** of tadpoles, frogs, and fish in the water.

A grass snake usually swims with its head out of the water.

GRASS SNAKE

BODY LENGTH:
27–47 IN. (70–120 CM)

WEIGHT:
3–11 OZ (90–300 G)

LIFESPAN:
UP TO 15 YEARS

HABITAT:
RIVERBANKS, PONDS, DITCHES

THAT'S AMAZING!:
GRASS SNAKES **HIBERNATE** FROM OCTOBER TO MARCH UNDER TREE ROOTS OR IN OLD RABBIT **BURROWS**.

where grass snakes live

North Sea

Atlantic Ocean

Europe

Mediterranean Sea

A grass snake can play dead for half an hour or more.

Grass snake defenses

Grass snakes are eaten by badgers, foxes, and hedgehogs. If a snake is in danger, it puffs up its body and hisses loudly to frighten off its attacker. If this does not work, it squirts out a foul-smelling liquid. If this also fails, the snake rolls over on its back and pretends to be dead. It stays completely still with its mouth open and its tongue hanging out until its attacker loses interest.

European Eel

European eels are long, narrow fish that spend part of their lives in the ocean and part in rivers. They make an extraordinary journey between their two **habitats**.

EUROPEAN EEL

BODY LENGTH:
8–31 IN. (20–80 CM)

WEIGHT:
UP TO 14.5 LBS (6.5 KG)

LIFESPAN:
85 YEARS

HABITAT:
RIVERS, SEA

THAT'S AMAZING!:
ON THEIR LONG JOURNEY, THE EELS CAN SURVIVE FOR SEVERAL HOURS OUT OF WATER AS THEY TRAVEL OVER LAND.

where European eels live

North Sea

Atlantic Ocean

Europe

Mediterranean Sea

Young eels are called glass eels because their bodies are see-through.

Eel lives

An eel lays its eggs in the Sargasso Sea, in the Atlantic Ocean. The eggs hatch into **larvae** that look like curled leaves. For up to three years, they drift on the ocean currents toward the coast. Then they turn into young eels that swim up rivers and spend up to 20 years growing into adults. As adults, they travel thousands of miles back to the sea to lay their eggs.

An adult eel's coloring makes it difficult for **predators**, such as sea birds, to spot it.

Changing color

As the eels grow, they change color to match their changing habitat. In rivers, they turn brown or yellow to match the muddy water. They turn silvery-gray to blend in with the sea.

Animals in Danger

Many animals in Europe are in danger of dying out. When an animal dies out, it is said to be **extinct**. Many animals are dying out because people are destroying their **habitats**, capturing them for pets, or killing them for their skins, meat, and body parts.

The osprey is a rare **bird of prey** that lives near lakes, rivers, and the sea. In the past, ospreys were shot by fish farmers because the birds ate the farmers' fish. Their nest sites were also destroyed and their eggs were stolen by egg collectors. Today, ospreys are being reintroduced to specially protected nesting sites and their numbers are growing.

Ospreys feed mainly on fish. They plunge into the water to catch prey.

The Spanish lynx used to be found throughout Spain and Portugal. It now only lives in a few forests in southern Spain. Much of its habitat has been destroyed to make room for building homes and hotels. The lynx hunts wild rabbits but many rabbits are being killed by disease. This is another threat to the lynx.

Today, **conservation** groups are working hard to save these amazing animals.

The Spanish lynx is one of the rarest cats in the world. There are only a few hundred left in the wild.

Animal Facts and Figures

There are millions of different types of animals living all over the world. The place where an animal lives is called its **habitat**. Animals have special features, such as wings, claws, and fins. These features allow animals to survive in their habitats. Which animal do you think is the most amazing?

WILD BOAR

BODY LENGTH:
5–6 FT. (1.5–1.8 M)

WEIGHT:
100–450 LBS (50–200 KG)

LIFESPAN:
15–20 YEARS

HABITAT:
WOODLANDS

THAT'S AMAZING!:
WILD BOARS LOVE TO WALLOW IN MUD POOLS. THEY DO THIS TO COOL DOWN AND GET RID OF IRRITATING **INSECTS**.

STAG BEETLE

BODY LENGTH:
1–3 IN. (2.5–7.5 CM)

WEIGHT:
ABOUT 0.07 OZ (2 G)

LIFESPAN:
UP TO 7 YEARS

HABITAT:
WOODLANDS

THAT'S AMAZING!:
A STAG BEETLE'S GIANT JAWS ARE USELESS FOR CHEWING. SCIENTISTS ARE NOT SURE IF ADULT STAG BEETLES EAT ANYTHING AT ALL.

NOCTULE BAT

BODY LENGTH:
2–3 IN. (6–8 CM)

WEIGHT:
0.6–1.4 OZ (18–40 G)

LIFESPAN:
UP TO 12 YEARS

HABITAT:
WOODLANDS

THAT'S AMAZING!:
A BABY NOCTULE BAT CAN FLY WHEN IT IS FOUR WEEKS OLD.

EUROPEAN EAGLE OWL

BODY LENGTH:
27 IN. (70 CM)

WEIGHT:
9 LBS (4.1 KG)

LIFESPAN:
UP TO 40 YEARS

HABITAT:
WOODLANDS, ROCKY AREAS

THAT'S AMAZING!:
HOURS AFTER AN OWL HAS EATEN A MEAL, IT VOMITS UP A PELLET OF BONES AND OTHER PIECES OF ITS PREY THAT IT CANNOT DIGEST.

ALPINE SALAMANDER

BODY LENGTH:
3.5–5.5 IN (9–14 CM)

WEIGHT:
0.5 OZ (15 G)

LIFESPAN:
10 YEARS

HABITAT:
MOUNTAINS

THAT'S AMAZING!:
TO AVOID THE COLD WEATHER AND LACK OF FOOD IN WINTER, ALPINE SALAMANDERS **HIBERNATE** FOR 6–8 MONTHS OF THE YEAR.

ALPINE MARMOT

BODY LENGTH:
20–28 IN. (53–73 CM)

WEIGHT:
9–18 LBS (4–8 KG)

LIFESPAN:
4–5 YEARS

HABITAT:
MOUNTAINS

THAT'S AMAZING!:
ALPINE MARMOTS WARN EACH OTHER OF DANGER, SUCH AS EAGLES OR FOXES NEARBY, BY WHISTLING A WARNING.

MIDWIFE TOAD

BODY LENGTH:
UP TO 1.5 IN. (38 MM)

LIFESPAN:
10 YEARS

HABITAT:
MOUNTAINS

THAT'S AMAZING!:
THE TOAD'S BACK IS COVERED IN SMALL WARTS. THE WARTS GIVE OFF A STRONG-SMELLING POISON IF THE TOAD IS ATTACKED.

PEREGRINE FALCON

BODY LENGTH:
13–20 IN. (34–50 CM)

WEIGHT:
1–3 LBS (0.5–1.5 KG)

LIFESPAN:
15 YEARS

HABITAT:
MARSHES, FARMLAND, ROCKY SEA COASTS

THAT'S AMAZING!:
PEREGRINES **MATE** FOR LIFE AND RETURN TO THE SAME NESTING SITE YEAR AFTER YEAR.

GRASS SNAKE

BODY LENGTH:
27–47 IN. (70–120 CM)

WEIGHT:
3–11 OZ (90–300 G)

LIFESPAN:
UP TO 15 YEARS

HABITAT:
RIVER BANKS, PONDS, DITCHES

THAT'S AMAZING!:
GRASS SNAKES **HIBERNATE** FROM OCTOBER TO MARCH UNDER TREE ROOTS OR IN OLD RABBIT **BURROWS**.

EUROPEAN EEL

BODY LENGTH:
8–31 IN. (20–80 CM)

WEIGHT:
UP TO 14.5 LBS (6.5 KG)

LIFESPAN:
85 YEARS

HABITAT:
RIVERS, SEA

THAT'S AMAZING!:
ON THEIR LONG JOURNEY, THE EELS CAN SURVIVE FOR SEVERAL HOURS OUT OF WATER AS THEY TRAVEL OVER LAND.

Find Out More

Books to read

Bingham, Jane. *Exploring Continents: Exploring Europe*. Chicago: Heinemann Library, 2007.

Parker, Steve. *Life Processes: Adaptation*. Chicago: Heinemann Library, 2007.

Parker, Steve. *Life Processes: Survival and Change*. Chicago: Heinemann Library, 2007.

Websites

http://animaldiversity.ummz.umich.edu
The Animal Diversity Web is run by the University of Michigan and features an extensive encyclopedia of animals.

http://animals.nationalgeographic.com/animals
This website features detailed information on various animals, stories of survival in different habitats, and stunning photo galleries.

http://www.bbc.co.uk/nature/reallywild
Type in the name of the animal you want to learn about and find a page with several facts, figures, and pictures.

http://www.mnh.si.edu
The website of the Smithsonian National Museum of Natural History, which has one of the largest natural history collections in the world.

Zoo sites
Many zoos around the world have their own websites that tell you about the animals they keep, where they come from, and how they are cared for.

Glossary

adapted when an animal has special features that help it survive in its habitat

amphibian animal, such as a toad or frog, that lives both on land and in the water

bird of prey bird that hunts for food using its talons

broadleaved trees, such as oaks and elms, that have wide leaves

burrow hole in the ground where an animal takes shelter

camouflage when an animal has special colors or markings that help it hide in its habitat

conservation saving and protecting wild animals and their habitats

continent one of seven huge pieces of land on Earth. Each continent is divided into smaller regions called countries.

dawn when the sun rises in the morning

dusk when the sun sets in the evening

extinct when a type of animal dies out forever

fungi mushrooms, toadstools, and molds

habitat place where an animal lives and feeds

hibernate to go into a deep sleep during winter

insect animal with six legs and three parts to its body

larvae grub-like young of insects

mate when an animal makes babies with another animal

nutrient substance found in the environment that animals need to grow and survive

predator animal that hunts and kills other animals for food

prey animal that is hunted and killed by other animals for food

talon bird's large, curved claw

woodland forest in which the trees are mostly broadleaved and deciduous (lose their leaves in winter)

Index